Empath Healing

Emotional Healing & Survival Guide for Empaths and Highly Sensitive People

by

Marianne Gracie

The information in the following pages is broadly considered to be a truthful and accurate account of facts and as such any inattention, use or misuse of the information in question by the reader will render any resulting actions solely under their purview. There are no scenarios in which the publisher or the original author of this work can be in any fashion deemed liable for any hardship or damages that may befall them after undertaking information described herein.

Additionally, the information in the following pages is intended only for informational purposes and should thus be thought of as universal. As befitting its nature, it is presented without assurance regarding its prolonged validity or interim quality. Trademarks that are mentioned are done without written consent and can in no way be considered an endorsement from the trademark holder.

Table of Contents

Preface

Dear Reader,

I just wanted to share a quick word before you dive into this book. I would like to start by saying thank you for taking the time to purchase this title. Every effort was taken to ensure it was written to a high standard with great information which should hopefully help empower you on this life journey. Sometimes we feel that we need a little extra motivation or to hear from someone who has been through a similar experience to ourselves, reading about other people's journeys can help empower us on ours. That was the real intention behind writing this book, even if it helps one person then I achieved what I set out to do. It has been written from my own personal struggles through life with being an empath and overly sensitive. But, once I learnt how to turn this around and harness the gift that it truly was, that was when my life began to change. I hope you have a similar realization in the following pages.

Thank you!

Marianne Gracie (Author)

MARIANNE GRACIE

Introduction

If you are reading this book, I am assuming that you either know you are an Empath, you're still trying to figure it out or know someone who is. Either way, you have come to the right place to help expand your knowledge as this book contains the most up to date information available on the subject.

The very first thing anyone who is interested in this topic should come to understand, is that this trait is part of an empaths genetic make-up. It will be with them for their whole life. It was likely inherited from one or even both parents. It is not an illness, disease or psychological disorder which can be treated by medicine or therapy.

But do not worry, you're not alone. Statistics have pointed out that around 1 in 20 people are also empaths or highly sensitive individuals. If you're an empath and have picked up this book to find a solution to this 'condition', then I am afraid you won't find one. With that said, the purpose of this book is to teach the empath exactly how to manage this trait effectively so they can reap the benefits of this gift while creating a happier future for themselves.

Along with empaths, there is another group of people who are commonly called Highly Sensitive People (HSP). For the purpose of this book, these two terms will be used interchangeably. Although I do understand some believe there is a difference between the two. The knowledge in this book will work for either Empaths or HSP's. Both types possess a heightened sense of feeling. That is the basis of which this book tackles the topic of feeling and sensitivity. So, do not be put off if you have classified yourself as a different term, this book provides information and knowledge for a range of related subjects.

The main purpose of this book is to help people begin to see that this attribute is a gift to the world and not a hindrance. Unfortunately, we have never been shown how to harness this attribute and work with it. Like anything in life, when we don't fully understand something, it can leave us feeling confused or fearful.

Having grown up with this trait and always feeling different from others, I have personally experienced many lows. It was only until I realized that I had to learn more about myself and how to accept all parts of me, that I was able to harness the true power which resides in being an Empath. Now I see it as special gift, something which many others do not have and can never have. Learning how to use this trait has enabled me to have and experience better relationships because I can understand others better without getting caught up in their emotions (something I struggled with most of my life).

Before this, I would often be left feeling drained from other people and certain environments I found myself in. After eventually becoming tired of being dragged down, I spent many years living alone so I wouldn't have to face the energy drainage of others. But, over time I realized that cutting myself of like this, wasn't beneficial for me or the world. I had a gift which I should be sharing and empowering others with. So I began to work, study and learn new ways I could go out into the world as a strong empath and use my abilities for good.

After a short time of educating myself, I discovered tools and techniques which would help me to thrive. I learnt ways to hold my energy so I could go out into the world and not be overwhelmed by others. This in turn, would allow me to make better decisions and experience less anxiety, which ultimately lead to a more fulfilled life.

How effectively we can connect with others, is one of the main factors of how much happiness we will experience in life. I agree, that empaths may be at a disadvantage at the beginning but from my own experience and other people I have worked with, what seems like a disability can be transformed into an incredible gift, with which empaths are able to connect with others much more effectively than most people can. Empathy is a communication tool, which allows us to become great communicators by understanding others on a much deeper level. Learning how to work with this will open so many doors for you.

This title will start by looking at empaths and the problems they face in greater detail. With these new understandings, we are able uncover emotional pain from years of living in this way. This wounding must be healed first if we are to move forward and positively impact the future of our lives. Here we will look at various methods of healing and overcoming past traumas. Along with this, the book contains a survival guide about all the tools empaths have at their disposal to be able to function at their best, while keeping anxiety, negativity and fear at bay. Many of the practical exercises in this book have been broken down in easy to understand chucks which can be implemented almost immediately.

The other facets empaths and sensitives must deal with are overwhelming environments such as crowded places and the energy of the planet. With so much negativity in the world, empaths must find a way to rise above it. In our inner journey of learning how to conquer and harness this natural feeling ability, we become accustomed and prepared to help tackle the problems people are facing in our world. An empaths life mission therefore, is of the highest purpose. Never forget this, it's this very reason that will help keep you strong!

What is an Empath?

Empathy – the capability to understand another's emotions.

Everyone is empathic, we all have a natural ability to feel, understand and relate to others. It is what makes us human and is a natural part of our hereditary make-up. Empathy is identifying with the other person, but everyone experiences varying degrees of this. Some people feel very little empathy, these people can suffer from psychological disorders such as sociopaths and psychopaths. Feeling a healthy degree of empathy is normal and a benchmark of a balanced personality. However, empaths are on the higher end of the spectrum - they feel too much, this makes the trait difficult to manage. Without knowing how to handle it, they can often be left feeling overwhelmed by their surroundings, particularly social situations or crowded places. They tend to overly-identify with people they come into contact with because they unconsciously pickup too much energy and emotion from them. This can become incredibly draining and not to mention very confusing, as they feel what others are feeling.

At the most fundamental level, everything in the world, living or otherwise, is made of energy. Each type of energy has a certain vibrational frequency. An empath has a sophisticated psychic ability to emotionally tune into the energetic experience of other people, certain places and even animals.

Empaths and HSP's can often pick-up on what others are thinking even before anything is said due to this natural sensitivity. Their skills go further than this however, as they are also great at reading others through body language, tone of voice, movements and thoughts, these abilities give them the natural skills to become great communicators.

Empaths sense and feel unseen energies of any situation or experience. For example, they may enter a room where an argument has just taken place and will often feel the presence of a foul energy. They can detect this through the energetic residue left in the room from the argument, this promotes their innate ability of natural intuitiveness. Often unconsciously, sensitives will experience good or bad vibes about a person or place. They also possess a natural creative flair, which they can express in various forms through their great imaginations and natural charisma, this is what draws others towards them.

From all these listed benefits, it might sound like being an Empath is ideal and something everyone should aspire too, but unfortunately all these positive attributes are balanced with some not so desirable qualities.

A sensitive person feels much more deeply than someone who doesn't have this natural tendency. Empathic people can be so sensitive, that they often unconsciously absorb others energies into their own bodies, this causes them to feel other people's emotions very deeply. Because of this, they often become confused and struggle to identify their own emotional needs and wants, as they're so overwhelmed by other people's feelings. This translates into the natural skills of nurturing and listening with compassion, consideration and a deep understanding of others. They are able to feel others pain and understand them more deeply because they've had a direct experience of their emotions. This attracts people to them, like a moth to a flame, people will often leave an interaction with an empath feeling much better. Animals are also naturally drawn to the energy of empaths.

Sensitive people are usually the ones, whom their friends turn to for help and advice. They will often go out of their way to help others and sacrifice their own needs in the process. For these reasons, it is incredibly important that empaths discover ways to protect themselves from taking on too much energy from others. People who 'dump' their negativity onto empaths, usually sense on some level that they feel better after speaking to an empath. Therefore, they continue to do it, it can almost become a form of psychic abuse. A major downside of having heightened empathic abilities is the development of weak or non-existent boundaries, finding it hard to say no because they've taken on others pain as their own.

HSPs and empaths can struggle to notice the difference between physical stress and energetic stress. For instance, when they have to make an effort to be more sociable this tends to tire them out physically because they're constantly bombarded with energetic stimulus from all around, it takes longer to process everything coming in. You may often feel worn out from meeting many new people at once or from being exposed to a new place or environment.

All words hold an energetic pattern, this frequency is taken on by the person who is speaking, reading or thinking these words. Words contain a meaning for us and each one carries a comparable emotional signature. When certain words are spoken they naturally evoke an emotional response. For example, strong words such as love and hate, contain within them the energetic meaning of the word. The person who therefore, is reading, thinking or talking about love, adds their emotion to the already powerful word. An empath can pick up on this subtle energy even though it wasn't the speakers intention. They're so naturally attuned to their energetic atmosphere that they cannot help but feel everything.

Empaths have so much power that they need to find ways in which to harness it by first learning to shield and protect themselves from unwanted energies. Once this goal is attained they are able to go out into the world in a bubble of protection and do amazing work to help heal and lift the planet to a higher vibration.

Sensitives can be found throughout the world, among all cultures and religions. In some cases, they can be found living alone, in a very quiet, depressed or neurotic lifestyle. Becoming a loner is an easy way out. Without learning how to protect their space, some are forced to live alone as being around others is just too tiresome and draining. So they like to spend time in solitude and nature can become a favorite ally. Here they find that the Earth is naturally grounding and recharges their overstimulated nervous system. Nature therefore becomes a powerful tool in the life of an empath.

Why am I like this?

Many empaths whom I have come into contact with, ask the same question - why have I been lumbered with this trait? In modern society, being extroverted and out-going is seen as something to aspire to and how 'normal' healthy people should behave. But empaths are naturally introverted, so trying to fit the mold of modern society can leave us feeling out of place and thinking there is something inherently wrong with us. It is important to recognize that there is nothing wrong with you and that you're not alone!

For most of my adult life I believed that my sensitivity was something psychological which I had picked up during my childhood. Following this I went through many years of therapy and self-exploration to eventually understand that it wasn't something I was able to get away from. It was a part of me. Genetically hardwired into my entire system. Once we come to this realization, we can then begin to accept and work with it.

Although there hasn't been much physiological research conducted to examine the causes of heightened sensitivity, here is some information to help give you a slightly better understanding of why you are this way. On a biological level, the reason empaths feel more deeply is due to a 'unique variation' in the workings of their central nervous system. Empaths have a much more sensitive nervous system when compared to non-empaths, this is what causes the sensations of being overwhelmed. Our nervous systems are picking up on everything from the environment and people around us. Due to this heightened sensitivity, empaths will also experience physical pain more deeply. As I child, I remember I hated washing my hair because I couldn't stand the water over my head. I couldn't enjoy children's swings and rides because the stimulation was just too much for me to take. I felt everything more deeply, I would even go red in the face through embarrassment very easily. Plain and simple – Empaths feel everything more!

This overly sensitive nervous system is usually genetic and is often passed down from one of the parents. To help improve our understanding of the physical reasons of this phenomenon we will take a brief over view of how the nervous system works and its purpose in helping us function.

The Nervous System

What is it? On a very basic level, it is the control center of our bodies – controlling all physiological and psychological reactions. It is made up of 2 parts – the central and peripheral nervous system. The central nervous system is comprised of the brain and spinal cord. The peripheral nervous system consists of many nerves spread throughout the body which enable us to engage our five senses. These nerves all feed into and are extensions of the central nervous system.

It is the most powerful system of the human body due to its control of our bodily senses, without it we wouldn't be able function. It allows us to feel heat and cold. When we feel hungry, messages are sent via the nerves to our brains to signal we need food. All these external and internal messages are processed by electrical and chemical signals which come to and from our nerve cells.

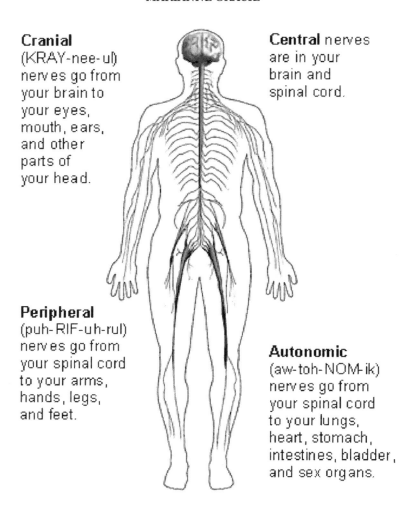

Cranial
(KRAY-nee-ul)
nerves go from
your brain to
your eyes,
mouth, ears,
and other
parts of
your head.

Central nerves
are in your
brain and
spinal cord.

Peripheral
(puh-RIF-uh-rul)
nerves go from
your spinal cord
to your arms,
hands, legs,
and feet.

Autonomic
(aw-toh-NOM-ik)
nerves go from
your spinal cord
to your lungs,
heart, stomach,
intestines, bladder,
and sex organs.

It is not clear whether both the central and peripheral nervous systems are highly sensitized. Or if it is only one part. But as we understand, the peripheral nervous system is responsible for the many nerves which travel throughout the body, this part will most certainly be highly sensitized, as it is what connects us to our reality. It is very likely the brain will also be, especially when we consider, sensitives respond more to certain stimulants and depressants (such as caffeine and alcohol) which work directly on the brain. If you have noticed getting drunk easily or caffeine has a big impact on you then it's extremely likely your brain is highly sensitized also.

In later chapters, we will look at what dietary habits and exercises you can incorporate into your life to help physically calm the nervous system. This should allow you to feel more grounded and more in control of yourself and your environment.

Global Energy

Not only must we begin to work to protect against others energy, who intrude on our boundaries but also protect against global waves of unconscious emotions such as fear, which are produced through negativity. When the negativity on our Planet is high, it is easily picked up by sensitives which can then cause further anxiety, this can make us feel very heavy and have a pounding like effect on us.

It is difficult to quantify when the energetic frequency of the planet is negative since we have no instruments to measure it. But we must use this gift, our sixth sense to sense it. By using our intuition, you can help promote harmony and healing around yourself, your loved ones and the planet.

If for instance, wars or political disputes are on-going, that have divided and created tension between large groups of people, there is no way of avoiding these collective forces of energy. Most people are unconscious of the energy created by large populations of people but empaths can become aware and begin to move themselves above it. This is achieved by protecting ourselves and having a positive impact on the people and environment around us (exactly how to do this will be discussed in later chapters). Empaths are needed on this planet to help balance these negative energies. It can feel like a challenge and we may ask why we have been lumbered with this task but this is the way it is. We can promote positivity on the planet in many ways even through little tasks such as helping others, promoting peace, creating positive content such as videos, blogs, articles and pictures, to name but a few.

Social anxiety and the Empath

Anxiety robs us of vital life energy. This unwanted psychological thought pattern consumes a significant part of our minds energy which we could use more productively to enhance our lives.

Without consciously taking control over themselves, empaths are open to everything. They have no protection. Research has proven that people who suffer from social anxiety are much more exposed to other people's emotional states. This sensitivity causes physical sensations within the body which is referred to as anxiety.

A 2011 study (1) proved people who suffer from social phobias were hypersensitive to other people's mind states and thoughts. The anxiety ridden participants were able to accurately perceive the feelings and thoughts of others in their close vicinity. This essentially proved that empathy is a gift as the volunteers were able to determine others emotional states just from being in their presence.

However, the downside of this psychic gift was that others emotions and energies was so distressing for the participants, that their brains would create anxiety feelings in the body in order to protect itself from what the researchers referred to as 'emotional pollution'. If your anxiety leads to panic attacks this can cause empaths to take on other states in an attempt to keep the panic attacks at bay. These include OCD, not leaving the house and depression, to name but a few.

Other sources of evidence have proven that empathy is impaired or even reduced in people who suffer from depression. This could mean that empaths may unconsciously retreat into depression in an attempt to block their natural empathic abilities. They may see this as the only real solution to stop themselves from being overwhelmed by others and their environment. Depression is effectively a cognitive dissonance, where the suffer denies or represses their own feelings, whether negative or positive. More on this later.

Anxiety – The empaths ability to effortlessly pick up subtle energies and emotions of their environment leaves them overwhelmed by too much extrasensory input. This overload causes people to panic when it becomes too much. The whole system feels like it is being bombarded with information and energy. This creates feelings of inadequacy within us because when we look around and see everyone else functioning fine, it makes us feel like we're the only ones who are so distressed. By seeing others functioning 'normally', we make the assumption that they either feel like we do and are still able to be effective or that they feel different from us, either way this enforces the belief that we must be either weird or strange. This type of thinking sends the message to ourselves that something is inherently wrong with us. Years of this type of programming, is incredibly harmful to an empaths self-esteem.

Empaths will look to the future if they are often left distressed with anxiety which creates more dis-ease since they are being pulled out of the present moment. It is not uncommon to suffer from intense anxiety, with a belief that something bad is going to happen at any moment. Whether they are going out with friends, out shopping, out riding in a car, or wherever it is, they are often accompanied by high levels of fear. Feeling like this essentially takes any pleasure out of living.

An evolved way to begin to look at this problem is first recognizing that these thoughts are not giving us what we need. We must find another healthier way to live. The anxious feelings are coming from our environment and from our unresolved emotional issues which are being expressed through dysfunctional thought patterns. The non-stop over anxious feelings are one big manifestation of all our fears which need to be purged. All anxiety and negative feelings need to be processed. When there is so much ego energy and self-loathing in others, like with the general unconscious population, this is easily picked up and transferred to sensitives.

I used to trick myself into believing that my anxious feelings were keeping me safe and without them I would end up in fearful circumstances. I would make logical arguments to myself to justify feeling worried all of the time. In the end, what I discovered was that I lacked belief in myself. If I had a healthy sense of self-esteem then no matter what life presented me with, I would be able to handle it because I was competent and capable. These positive beliefs can only come from a healthy sense of self-esteem and confidence. That is why self-love crushes any type of anxiety, if gives us the belief we can handle life.

For empaths who are familiar with the law of attraction, it is important to understand that when we are full of fear and anxious, then vibrationally we are unable to attract the things we want into our lives. We only bring in what matches our vibration. It is of no surprising then if it sometimes feels like we are struggling to move forward. We must change ourselves first before our world can reflect this back to us. Living in fear, anxiety and worry will only bring more of this into our lives. The hard truth is that empaths will find it more challenging to change since they must deal with not only their own issues, but the compounded burden of over stimulation. Of course, this makes it more difficult, but at the same time, much more worthwhile. The high empaths can feel once they have conquered themselves is unparalleled.

Intimacy

Intimacy is the basis of close relationships. It essentially means allowing another to get close enough to us, to see all of our darkest secrets and flaws. Sharing our emotional feelings with another creates an emotional bond between us. This can only be achieved by letting go of and releasing any defenses which we had previously held in place to help keep us safe.

Experiencing true intimacy can be incredibly challenging for many people. But none more so than for Empaths. This word intimacy has been famously broken down into the phrase *'Into me you see'*. When we take into account all the pain and heartbreak we have had to endure through life it is easier to understand why being seen closely 'warts and all' can be so terrifying.

In defense of being exposed to others, we put up walls to protect us, but these walls shut off our feelings and keep our true self hidden away. These walls can take form through various methods such as attracting the wrong partners, avoiding close relationships or becoming a social outcast, a loner. We often convince ourselves that we are doing the right thing but our resulting actions usually come from a place of fear. The fear that our deepest flaws will be exposed and we will be seen as inadequate.

It is not uncommon that empaths will remain single their whole life, since they like to be alone so much as they don't have to feel others stresses and emotions. Often times they become so accustomed to spending time alone that they don't feel lonely anymore but this is not incredibly healthy. Empaths should understand that they are capable of healthy relationships providing respectful boundaries can be established between partners.

To achieve this we must learn to make ourselves vulnerable again and trust that we are equipped enough to deal with whatever comes our way. This is the mark of the fully mature person.

In an authentically intimate relationship, all of our fears can be brought out into the light of love and be examined. This is one of the greatest benefits of relationships, they allow us to share ourselves with another and grow together. When there is little genuine intimacy within a relationship then self-doubts and insecurities can creep in, these effectively put the partnership under immense strain. Romantic relationships have a knack of exposing our deepest flaws and insecurities but instead of running from them, we need to hold and understand them to eventually free ourselves.

Healthy intimacy also comes from learning to look within ourselves, *'Into me I see'*. When we develop the courage to truly look at ourselves we learn to gradually accept our fears and faults. This in turn allows us to let others closer. By befriending ourselves, we can then befriend others. Intimacy is also the foundation of social relations, without it there is no real spark when meeting new people. Yes, the people you meet will probably feel comfortable unloading all of their issues onto you, because of your empathic nature, but a genuine connection will remain elusive without a real emotional bond.

This rings true for all our relationships. For example, I have a son and I always had the sense that I wasn't fully connecting with him. He is also an empath, this wasn't something I had discussed with him until he was much older but I was able to see how it had passed down from me to him. I could see it in his traits and behaviors. He is so kind and caring to others. Never any trouble to anyone and like many other empaths, he spends a lot of time on his own. But once I was able to open up and get deeply in touch with my own reservoir of feelings, I was able to get in contact with his feelings. Our children need to feel an emotional connection from us. This is how they learn to get in touch with their own feelings. This will determine if our children will go onto live happy successful lives. Once they feel our deep unconditional love for them, it allows them to open up.

Unfortunately intimacy isn't something which can be found overnight, it comes to us gradually by learning to let go of any resistance and fears by softly opening up to our self and others. Doing this slowly will begin to move you into the right direction for healthy growth and relationships. Start this process by learning to accept yourself just as you are, right now.

Empaths and Intimacy

Empaths often suffer problems in maintaining healthy relationships. I believe this is down to our heightened sensing ability. As children, our feelings were felt too deeply and this was overwhelming or even painful for us. To protect ourselves from these heavy emotions we closed ourselves off out of fear of experiencing pain again. But by blocking out the painful feelings, we obstructed our positive feelings at the same time. The human mind is not logical, it doesn't understand good and bad. If we decide to block our painful feelings, the mind is unable to differentiate between what we want and don't want.

Repression, requires a lot of our psychological energy and we end up blocking much more than just the unwanted stuff but other rich aspects of our personalities too. For instance, by repressing our desire to be seen, we may also lose a natural talent to communicate well. It is almost impossible to only repress one facet of ourselves and avoid others because our traits and feelings are interconnected. If you repress one aspect of yourself, you will inevitably push others away also.

Learning to repress themselves from a young age, sends the young empath within and often into shyness especially if they've experienced too much pain. Then out of fear of feeling again, the empath creates further psychological blocks to help protect themselves.

Life is often even more difficult for the youngster if they grew up in a dysfunctional household witnessing physical, emotional or mental abuse. All of this combined negative energetic stimulus forces the empath to close themselves off from a very young age. As they grow up, they often struggle to reach out and connect with others because of the defense mechanisms they developed earlier in life. Their heightened sensitivity increases any painful feelings, which are almost unbearable for a young child. So, their true self goes into hiding.

I grew up with two sisters in a somewhat dysfunctional family. I do believe my sisters have a certain degree of sensitivity also, but not to the degree which I always have. Anything which happens in the household, is felt and picked up more by the most sensitive child, so the long-term impact they have to deal with is greater too. Empaths feel all experiences much deeper. But, by becoming aware of your natural tendencies you can work to protect and better equip yourself from future psychological and emotional damage. With that said, the painful wounds of childhood will need healing also.

By pushing their feelings and their needs for emotional connection away, these are repressed down into the unconscious psyche. Repression of any feelings doesn't mean that is the end of them. Since all emotions are energy, they cannot be destroyed but only converted. Repressed emotions then come out in other ways, often as anxiety, stress or depression. Our feelings serve to guide us through life which helps give us direction and purpose. By cutting them off is almost like going through life blind, metaphorically speaking. These people will instead look outside of themselves for guidance because they're incapable of trusting their own feelings.

The solution to overcoming these issues, is to stop repressing your feelings while understanding it is safe for you to come out into the world by getting in touch with your emotions, desires and wants – Your true self! It is ok for you to have desires and needs, it is also perfectly acceptable to get these needs met just as much as anyone else's. Other people's needs should not gain priority over yours just because you feel theirs as well. That is what being a healthy mature adult is, owning your own feelings and getting your needs met. This can feel foreign to an empath at the beginning, but it is the first steps to taking ownership back of your Self.

If you have been spending a lot of time alone. You may be repressing your desire to truly connect with others in a healthy way. Human beings are social creatures and always have been.

No matter how shut off we sometimes feel, creating connections with others will often be the most fulfilling parts of our lives.

'Relationships are the hallmark of the mature person'
– Brain Tracy (Motivational Speaker) (2)

Since empaths learn from a young age to sit on their feelings, overtime they become masters at hiding how they feel without even knowingly realizing it. They're unconsciously still under the assumption that if they let someone close, the pain will be unbearable. But, we are grown now. We are not defenseless little children anymore and although we still feel deeply, we can handle and manage the pain better now due to our increased maturity, intellect, reasoning, education and life experiences.

It is ok to have needs. It is ok to have feelings. Let them out, allow yourself to experience them once again. Start to feel yourself again, is there pain there? What do you feel? (There is an exercise later which will take you through this whole process).

Close relationships leave empaths open to more hurt because they'll also pick-up their partners pain. Effectively doubling the heart ache. That is why being in a relationship with a partner who carries emotional wounding can hold the empath back from freeing themselves. In this scenario, they will energetically pick up their partner's pain, this is unavoidable due to the close proximity and connection they share. Then trying to clear and heal your own wounds becomes increasingly difficult.

The flip-side of this, is that empaths have the profound ability to feel love deeper than others. Feeling another's love can transform their whole lives. But first they must pluck up the courage and allow themselves to become vulnerable. The possibility of being able to feel genuine love from another should be the light which empaths follow, this will keep them warm on this frightening journey. The love you will feel at the end of this road will be worth the pain. Until you experience it, you will never know just how profound true love can feel for you.

Sexual Intimacy

Without genuine intimacy, sexual relationships suffer. A healthy emotional connection is the foundation of healthy sexual intimacy. This is why empaths often struggle with sexual dysfunction. We will now briefly look at some sexual issues which can be common in empaths.

Promiscuity - This involves having many casual sexual partners with no real intimate connection. It is not uncommon for empaths to fall under this category due to a lack of self-worth, they try to seek it through having sex with multiple partners. By behaving in this way, they feel some control over their lives as they can choose and control who they have sex with, this gives them a skewed sense of validation of their own worth. They also look for this validation from over performing sexually and then receiving compliments from their partners. This type of behavior can become incredibly addictive and the empath can start to derive all of their self-worth on their sexuality and therefore define themselves through this medium. This can lead to them boasting to others about their sexual prowess. Any such encounters are often followed by intense bouts of shame. On the opposite end of the scale, some empaths can move towards celibacy. Delving into deeper empathic sexual issues is beyond the scope of this book but it is worth remembering that this part of an empaths life is not always straight forward.

Once empaths can begin to feel the intensity of genuine non-physical intimacy it will usually be more profound than anything they had previously experienced physically. Sex is typically the closet an empath can come to another, but this physical closeness doesn't always translate to emotional closeness. This often leaves them feeling rather confused but being truly intimate is much deeper than just having sex. People generally feel sex is the closet they can get to another. But there are levels of deeper intimacy and sex which most people have never experienced, empathic or not.

For empaths to begin honoring themselves and their feelings, they should start becoming more protective of who they decide to share their sexual energy with. Since they want to give and help others, they can sometimes feel that giving sex is all they have to give. If you're an empath who's in a relationship, start to work on emotionally connecting with your partner more and put sex on the back-burner. Or, if dating a new partner, make them wait before you decide to have sex, although this can be difficult for empaths to do. Also, in modern day culture if people are not forth coming with their sexuality in relationships this is seen as something negative. The empaths goal should be to feel and honor themselves first and foremost.

Without genuine intimacy, empaths are unable to connect with their partner on a deeper level, this can often feel like hanging out with a friend as opposed to a being with someone you're deeply in love with. If your relationship feels more like a friendship, or a fake type of intimacy then try to understand this and learn how to deal with it.

The primary emotions include - love, joy, surprise, anger, sadness and fear. Most people are comfortable expressing at least a few of these. Sometimes the negative ones can be more difficult for empaths to get in touch with, especially anger. Since they are so aware and cautious of upsetting others, this can cause them to repress negative emotions such as anger or sadness. Pushing these powerful emotions away creates longer term psychological issues. Empaths often pride themselves on never getting angry. But repressing these feelings is energetically taxing which leads to this energy being expressed in other ways usually through depression, stress or anxiety.

When we isolate ourselves from others, we experience the same neuro chemicals in our bodies as when suffering from stress.

Only by getting in touch with yourself will you develop true inner strength, with this you can then begin to tolerate closeness and eventually start to enjoy it. It requires a lot of courage and introspection to really understand if we are in a healthy relationship or not. Being with someone who carries a lot of emotional pain causes a lot of damage to empaths. Although the other person will find it healing and helpful, it can be crippling for a sensitive.

Choosing the Right Partner

Childhood conditioning and past programming's often lead empaths to fall for the wrong person in relationships. But when they start getting more in tune with their self and feelings, the heart and soul naturally begin to align, with this alignment they start to see people who are emotionally available for healthy relationships while steering clear of the abusive and energy draining types. Since we attract what we essentially are, we must become emotionally healthy to have a truly wonderful and fulfilling relationship.

Taking time out from dating and relationships, can be beneficial in helping the empath to develop stronger emotional boundaries. Unfortunately, this won't happen overnight, especially since empaths have weak boundaries through years of letting others emotionally dump on them. Take the time to get in touch with your needs and from there decide what you are looking for from a relationship. Learning to love yourself fully and unconditionally first, will allow you to find someone who mirrors this back to you. This creates the foundation of a healthy intimate relationship. It is in these types of partnerships where the intensity of non-physical intimacy is more powerful than physical intimacy.

By allowing yourself to let go of past hurts you begin healing yourself, this frees you up to start enjoying each moment more and more until eventually you create a great feeling inside yourself, this makes it easier to create healthy connections with others. You are then in a powerful place of being able to consciously select the right partner. Sexual intimacy then becomes the icing on a magnificent cake, and not the whole cake itself.

Although empaths are great at knowing and reading others from their energetic and emotional presence, in close intimate relationships this can become increasingly difficult to do. This is because the emotional connection is sometimes too strong and it distorts the empaths ability to read their partners energy effectively. An empaths' sensing ability is similar to a highly-attuned instrument which works most optimally when others are at a certain emotional range from us. When we allow people too close, this attunement distorts the ability to read the other, which can lead to confusion and misunderstandings. Similar to when the frequency of a radio channel isn't quite tuned in and interference can be heard.

Empaths should learn to take relationships slowly. When they gradually figure the other person out, they can move the relationship to the next level. This creates its own challenges. Not everyone will be willing to take it slow. The partner of an empath must understand that the other person requires a certain amount of time alone. It is also generally believed that empaths have a better relationship with non-empaths as the opposites help to build a stronger partnership. Two empaths together can be a little overwhelming and it can likely be too much for both of them. That is not to suggest that it isn't possible.

Feeling Your Feelings

Here is a technique for getting more in-tune with any repressed feelings you have hidden away for a long time. These can be anxiety related, repressed emotions, or any wants and needs. It includes whatever you have not allowed a healthy expression. Most of the time we aren't even aware of what we repress. Use these processes either in real life situations or while visualizing events. I like to see this exercise as an act of mindful meditation.

1) The first step is to acknowledge the feeling.

When faced with an overwhelming situation which invokes a strong sense of emotion, such as anxiety, pay attention and acknowledge the sensation within your physical body. Whenever we are overcome by emotion this should act as an indicator that there is a potential for inner growth, even though it may make us want to run, flee or attack.

2) Make a conscious choice to stay with the physical sensation.

Do this by taking slow deep breathes, in through the nose and out through the mouth. Stay with the uncomfortable feeling with no resistance and clear mind.

3) Examine the feeling closely.

For example, if you experience nerves while public speaking, using this exercise you can coach yourself out of it. Visualize the event vividly in your mind, feel the bodily sensations you experience when speaking in public. This will cause the body to emotionally react as if the event is happening for real. Take your focus to the part of the body where these feelings of anxiety or discomfort are the most intense. It will usually be in the torso from your throat down to your groin region. Examine the physical sensation, really feel what it feels like. Pay close attention to it and its properties. What color is this feeling? How big is it? How heavy is it? Try to quantify this feeling as much as you can. You can even give it a name. Or call it your buddy, friend or anything which makes the sensation feel less threatening. This allows you to start connecting to and getting to know yourself.

4) Be in absolute non-resistance.

Allow the physical sensations to be, they are neutral, they mean nothing. Forget any thoughts which attach themselves to this feeling. We unconsciously attach thoughts to our feelings which then become our emotions. Instead of feeling the bodily sensation, we instead continually swirl related thoughts around our head over and over, this creates a hormonal response which sends our thoughts into overdrive and creates anxiety. The feeling and the thought have no connection apart from the one we have given it. When the feeling and the thought combine, that is what creates anxiety.

5) Set an intention

Once identifying where in the body this feeling is, set the intention to move it out of you. You can create goals for self-growth or of healing yourself. You can visualize how you will act when these negative feelings have left you.

6) Continue to stay with it for as long as possible while breathing deeply.

Over time the sensation in the body will begin to weaken and the related thoughts will also lessen. Until this happens continue to concentrate and focus intently. Breathe into these feelings. Breathe with them. Each emotion has an energetic signature, this is what you are looking for.

7) Go beyond your comfort zone

The bad feelings we feel, is what most people try to avoid through junk food, alcohol, drugs and TV. Most people cannot face themselves in this way. Overindulgence in anything is what stops us from feeling painful emotions and fears. They want to be processed and expressed but it is painful to do so. The pain of our feelings confronts us when we reach the limits of our comfort zone. Start to pay more attention to this and consciously try to go beyond what is comfortable for you.

8) The key to growth and transmuting old feelings and energies

By consciously pushing ourselves to go further, we delve deeper into our negative feelings. Then by learning to stay with them for long as possible through concentration and focus we eventually move through them. This is called non-resistance.

9) Very strong feelings

When coming across incredibly strong feelings, one thing you can do, is to physically let them out. Grab a pillow and scream into it. Let the feeling out from you. Scream as loud as possible. This screaming can last for a long or short time. Whatever feels right. Sometimes using emotionally moving music can help to move the feeling on. The body will essentially open up to allow the unwanted feelings to finally be processed.

Practice this regularly, on any unwanted emotions. Become more aware and notice what you're feeling in your body whenever you are overcome by a strong sensation or emotion. Try to forget about the thought and just concentrate on the feeling. This is a powerful transformational tool.

The long-term benefits of doing this exercise are immeasurable. The powerful intelligence which resides in unfelt feelings can blossom outward and enrich our mind, which enables us to see life from a brand-new perspective. To keep these feelings trapped, repressed and unprocessed (like we do for many years) comes at a heavy price. The cost was access to our inner gold and self-worth. This gold is a piece of our true self. A piece of our wisdom and inner strength. When we can release these unwanted feelings in a healthy way, we get back a wholeness and intelligence which we have always had, but most likely never experienced.

Setting Energetic Boundaries

Growing up in a relatively small town I never truly understood just how sensitive I was until later in life (even though I was painfully shy in my youth). My sensitivity was all that I had known and therefore I thought it was normal. In the back of my mind I always felt different from others but I wasn't able to pin-point why this was. When I reached my 30's however, I decided to move to a big city for a brand-new experience. As soon as I set foot into this new place I noticed a huge difference from where I had grown up. I could feel an energetic difference in the atmosphere. It just felt different and I really struggled to settle there. My body always felt on alert and I found it increasingly difficult to relax. For the first six months, I even struggled to sleep, as the energy of the place was much faster paced, then what I had been used to. Also, due to the much higher volumes of people, I couldn't go anywhere where I wasn't surrounded by others. By the end of the day I would feel completely worn out. Even though I would work to keep my own energy high, going out would eventually leave be feeling drained. This was because I hadn't learnt how to set energetic boundaries for myself, where I would be able to hold my own energy and stop others from infiltrating and intruding on my space. Evidentially, the people I would come into contact with day to day, would rob me of my high positive energy (which I had been working hard to maintain) and leave me with their low negative crappy energy. It is no real wonder I was worn out!

However, I learnt an awful lot from spending a year in a busy city, I finally understood myself to be an empath. Although I was tired most of the time it enabled me to finally learn how to hold my energy better and shield myself from others. It was the only way an empath could survive in a heavily populated place. Many big cities, are almost intrusive of personal space, especially on public transport. It is not energetically healthy for an empath or sensitive person to be in such close proximity to other people. They will easily pick up others energy in these environments unless they can learn to develop strong firm boundaries. If you are in public places often, then start to use these as practice in maintaining energetic boundaries. I would even suggest avoiding rush hours and extremely busy areas if possible, until you have developed firm enough boundaries to be able to handle these places.

How to Set Boundaries

Empaths have the problem of not being able to feel their own needs deeply enough because they are so overwhelmed by the feelings and wants of others. This is why they need to develop even stronger boundaries than a non-empathic person.

Their boundaries are far too permeable to others when they should instead be much firmer in order to provide them with a strong energetic foundation of support. Lacking adequate boundaries in our interactions with others, means we find it extremely difficult to say no, which can often lead to empaths being taken advantage of. One of the hardest things for an empath to understand (because of the way they are made to feel) is that it is not their job to make others happy. They must learn how to make themselves happy first.

The first step in creating healthier boundaries is by increasing your self-confidence. Most of us have been brought up and conditioned through society and by our caregivers that being agreeable means that we are well behaved and therefore good. With these types of beliefs, we often disown our own opinions which results in a lack of confidence. This is a violation against our true selves especially when we carry these types of beliefs into adulthood. Following the exercises in this book will help to improve your self-confidence, there are also countless sources available online for helping increase confidence.

The second step in setting a strong energetic boundary is to be in non-resistance to the other people we are protecting ourselves from. This can be initially quite difficult, especially if others have been infiltrating our space for some time. But without releasing this resistance, we will be unable to prevent them from breaking our boundaries again. It is easy to judge people who are impeding on us. By having an emotional reaction to and judging the people we are trying to keep out, we actually make it easier for them to penetrate our boundary again, which weakens it even further.

The next key to developing boundaries is to have a strong sense of grounding. This is essentially connecting our body to the Earths energy. The whole energetic area (about an arm's length all around you) should be connected to the Earth, not just the area which we cover physically.

1) Oils and Incense

Plant oils and incense sticks have been used for grounding for thousands of years. Herbs such as sage and cedar are still very popular to help cleanse a negative area while bringing positive energy into it. Sage in particular, which gives off a incense-like scent, is often used to clear negativity. Essential oils can also be used for the same purpose.

2) Water

Water could be described as an empaths best friend. It can be used in numerous ways to help with grounding. Taking a quick shower or bath has an incredible effect as it removes and neutralizes the empaths energy. You can even go out in the rain, go swimming, or just go and sit next to water. Adequate daily consumption of water is also highly recommended. Almost any use of water will have a positive grounding effect.

3) Walk barefoot

Probably the most common grounding technique out there and it's easy to do. Simply remove your shoes and walk on the Earth. It can be in your backyard, out in nature, on the beach or anywhere you feel comfortable. By physically feeling the Earth beneath your feet allows you to feel connected while helping to rebalance your emotional state.

Breathing Techniques for Protection

1) Find a quiet peaceful place. Get yourself into a centered and still mindset. Start by paying all of your attention onto your breath. Breathe in through your nose and out through your mouth.

2) When breathing out imagine creating a bubble around you. However far you envision your breath going out, is what defines your own personal space. Usually an arm's length radius is sufficient.

3) This bubble should encompass all around you, if there was someone close behind, you would easily detect their presence since your bubble is sensitive their energy.

4) Your bubble has the ability to expand and contract. For example, you can consciously make it expand when you're public speaking or at a party, or whenever you need to be expressive or seen. On the other hand, whenever you're are in a busy overwhelming environment or do not want to be noticed,

you can constrict your bubble and pull it in towards your body. This helps protect from being intruded upon by others.

5) During this process, you want to begin working with this bubble. As you breathe in, imagine this bubble pulling inward. But, when breathing outward imagine the bubble expanding. Learn to consciously control this boundary through visualization and through your breath.

6) Working consciously with your breath is the most important factor in this exercise. Focus on your breath whenever you feel you need protection from others or from an over stimulating environment.

7) Always visualize your bubble as a strong boundary which protects you easily. See it as clear with no tears or holes in it.

8) If you feel someone has infiltrated your area with their emotions or energy, during the exhale phase, imagine pushing this unwanted energy out and away from your space. By becoming more conscious of your own space, you will easily become aware when this bubble is penetrated against your wish. This can often be through a feeling or emotion.

9) With practice, you will feel and become aware of the presence of this protective bubble. This will enable you to work with and control it much easier.

10) Everyone has an aura or energy space around them but most people do not take responsibility for what they allow to enter this

space. Therefore, they often pick up things which do not belong to them. This technique works to protect your own positive energy by preventing others from robbing it from you or exchanging it for their negativity.

There is no right or wrong way to do this, if it feels right to you, it will serve its intended purpose. Feel free to alter parts of this process if you believe it works better.

Practice these boundary techniques as often as possible or until it becomes habitual. Then eventually you will unconsciously control your bubble of protection without even thinking about it. Reaching this point requires some dedication to the practice.

Without learning how to draw energetic boundaries our aura can become too expansive and project outward from us, up to many meters away. If for example, you have a garden full of animals, unless you build a fence around the garden the animals will roam away and you will likely lose most of them. In the same way, we need to build a metaphorical fence around us to contain our energy. If the aura projects too far outwards, let us say at a 5-meter radius all around, then we will pick up whatever is in that area. When out in public, that is potentially a lot of unwanted energy and things which can stick to us.

Without learning to control the aura through a firm boundary, some of our power and vital life energy is lost. But by making a conscious decision to reclaim your energy by pulling it in towards you significantly reduces any losses. The normal resting place for the aura or energy boundary should be close to the body, no more than an arms width radius. This boundary can be consciously expanded through breathwork and visualizing whenever you need to be seen or heard by others. Exercising to constrict and expand your boundary will strengthen your space and allow you more protection from others while also enabling you to be seen.

Healthy boundaries will also help empaths from losing their vital energy through cracks and leaks in the aura. This usually occurs in crowded public places, as our life force can be rapidly sucked away.

Tips for setting boundaries

Empath Meditation

Meditation should be the corner stone of building a healthy and happier life for an empath. It works to reset the mind and body. Sensitives can meditate while imaging themselves engulfed in a white bubble of light which is made of love and protection. Envision this bubble as something which keeps all negativity out. Similar to the grounding technique above, meditate with the aim to keep yourself guarded from unwanted things. The benefits of meditation are incredible, if you aren't meditating at the moment. Here is another good reason to start.

Scan and Check

Another handy tip for sensitives, is to scan their bodies through their attention and awareness before going out anywhere. By working to feel within your own body and checking for emotions or pains before going out, this will allow you to feel what is already there, in other words what is yours. Then when out of the house, you should be able to detect any different emotions or energies which were not present earlier. This is something you likely picked up from someone else.

Mantra

This is a quick and powerful way to create protection if you don't have the time to meditate or ground yourself. It involves creating a mantra for protection but holding a firm belief in its effectiveness is key. Create a mantra for yourself and memorize it so you can use it if and when you need it. An example, of a protection mantra could be something like *'I am encompassed in the light of love and protection. I am protected against any and all negative energies and their effects. Nothing negative can harm or affect me'.*

You can repeat this mantra in your head or silently to yourself if you feel particularly overwhelmed and feel the need for protection. Affirm this statement while keeping your intention within your body scanning for any physical sensations. This will naturally strengthen your energy and aura.

Block or not?

A final word on boundaries, most empaths will eventually learn how to block all external energy coming their way. Although this is a healthy way to tackle the situation for newly learned sensitives, longer-term this may not be the best solution. By blocking all external energies, we are also blocking positive messages coming our way. To live creatively and fully, we need to recognize what is going on around us. When setting the intention of creating a solid boundary it is beneficial to consciously decide to make it permeable to positive energy, only if you feel comfortable doing this. If you're new to setting energetic boundaries, then it would be best to stick with blocking all energies and then with expertise and time understand what you want to let in and what you do not.

Dietary Habits & Lifestyle Changes for Empaths

It is becoming increasingly evident that the foods we eat have a big impact on our psychological and physical state. This is even more relevant to a sensitive person. Firstly, we need to recognize that our physiology is slightly different from others so our bodies need caring for in different ways. By promoting our health and taking extra care, we can begin to better equip ourselves for the day ahead. If for example, you know you have to go to a business meeting and converse with others, this may usually lead to you feeling worn out by the end. But by preempting this event and making the necessary lifestyle choices, you can improve your ability to handle the situation without hitting a low afterwards. These changes will not only help you handle high stress situations, but feel more in control and allow you to return to normality much quicker. It is important to remember that empaths will usually have to develop new lifestyle habits so that they can experience long-term benefits.

Although Empaths and sensitives require more downtime than others to recover and regenerate themselves back to full energy, this shouldn't be confused with shutting oneself away and avoiding life and the world. Through managing your health, you can learn to thrive anywhere.

To begin we will look at some nutrients which empaths should include in their diet or through supplementation. Many of these work directly with the nervous system to help promote stability.

1) Magnesium

This is a very popular mineral which is needed for many bodily functions. It's particularly helpful when feeling stressed. Empaths naturally experience high levels of stress which uses up all of their magnesium reserves, this often causes them to become deficient in this vital mineral. Magnesium works as a relaxant which is important since sensitives carry a lot of muscular tension and stress in their bodies. Magnesium helps release any feelings of anxiety and depression by naturally allowing the body to relax, which also relives tension.

2) B-complex

Every time we are under strain the body uses this compound to help us cope with stress physiologically. B-complex also helps with anxiety, depression and irritability. B-vitamins play a key role in supporting the nervous system, cardiovascular system and are also beneficial in helping us digest food. Try to find a high-quality B-complex multi-vitamin to help make the nervous system more robust to the daily rigors of being an empath.

3) Valerian

This compound is an herbal medicinal plant. It works to reduce hyper sensitivity and irritability by nourishing the nervous system. It is especially effective after a stressful day. Its benefits include reducing anxiety, improving sleep while promoting stress management.

4) Vitamin C

This is popular vitamin can easily be found through eating a healthy diet. It is great for healing, repairing and boosting immune system function. Excess stress is related to sickness and ill health. Sensitives and empaths can use up their vitamin C stores very quickly if they experience high stress levels. What non-empaths may consider a moderate level of stress, can be considered a high-level of stress for some empaths.

5) Rescue medicine/remedy

This is made up of 5 different flower essences and is also known as a 'Flower Remedy'. Rescue remedy functions on the emotional level by helping restore emotional imbalances which can help us cope with various types of sensitive and stressful situations. It is great for helping with focus while reducing anxiety and depression. It is emotionally soothing.

Adrenal Gland Fatigue

The adrenal glands are situated just above the kidneys. The outer part of these glands, the adrenal cortex, is responsible for producing important hormones such as cortisol and others, these vital hormones work to help the body respond to stress while regulating our metabolism. Cortisol is most popularly known as the stress hormone which is secreted in abundance in response to any fearful situations, also known as the fight of flight response.

When an empath feels worn out and exhausted they can often suffer from adrenal fatigue. This occurs when the adrenal glands natural hormones (which help keep us upbeat and energized), become depleted through stress, anxiety, exhaustion and insomnia. All of these symptoms are very common in empaths, therefore so is adrenal fatigue.

By learning to manage adrenal fatigue we can begin to reverse these symptoms and gradually get a better handle on external stressors. Here are a few things you can do to help –

- Stay away from refined sugars and stimulants - These kick an already sensitive system into overdrive and causes the adrenals to work harder which leads to burnout. Try some fruit instead.
- Exercise - Regular exercise will help to cleanse and clear out your body and adrenals while also helping release any negative emotions you might have picked up.

- Sunlight and fresh air - Try to get out of a stuffy house or office and take in the fresh air and vitamin D from the sun. Both will help heal the adrenals.

Recharging Strategies

Now we will look at some general strategies which will help keep your energy clear and vibrant most of the time. By taking the time to work these practices into your daily life, you'll see a noticeable improvement in your overall health and well-being.

We have a natural ability to positively impact the world but our energy needs to vibrant and clear in order to be truly effective.

Sleep –

Probably the number one regenerative thing an empath can do is to get a good night's sleep, as often as possible. Due to their natural sensitivity, sleep is something we can often struggle with. I personally have certain requirements when it comes to sleeping well. First and foremost, the room must be pitch black with no visible light, secondly, I require it to be deadly silent so you cannot hear a pin drop and finally I need my own bed. Hotels or friends' houses are usually a struggle for me to sleep in. Pay attention to your own sleeping habits and what prerequisites you require.

Empaths need regular deep sleep to help regenerate back to full health. Through this they're able to recharge their sensitive system. If you struggle with sleep, try meditating just before going to bed. Stay away from any medication and sleeping pills as they create long-term sleeping issues due to reliance.

If you're like me, your phone is usually the last thing you look at before going to sleep and the first thing you check in the morning. This could actually be hindering your ability to get a good night's sleep. Research has suggested that the light given off by our electronic gadgets such as phones and tablets hinders the adequate release of the hormone melatonin, this is an important hormone in the regulation of healthy sleep patterns. The less you release the harder it will be to fall asleep. Again, the light of these electronics will most likely impact empaths and sensitives more. So, try switching these devices off at least one hour before you hit the sack.

I have personally found listening to a relaxing audiobook or some meditation music helps me to nod off naturally. Try to get to sleep by 10pm if possible. The human body functions just like the natural cycles of mother nature. Sleeping my 10pm optimizes our hormones and important chemicals which determine our energy levels, how we feel and our vitality. If we are out of synch with this cycle, we will pay the price.

Sleep deprivation for an empath can be very distressing. The importance of a good night's sleep cannot be overstated.

Sea Salt Bath -

When feeling overwhelmed or stressed, take the time to have a bath. Grab a few handfuls of sea salt and add it to your bath. The added salt will work to cleanse and revitalize your energy field by washing away any negative energy. Before getting in send an intention to the bath water, to cleanse you completely. Soak in the bath for at least half an hour.

Smoothies -

Eating and following a healthy lifestyle is very important for sensitives as we react badly to the additives and artificial ingredients added to a lot of food these day. A great healthy and tasty way to get more goodness into your diet is through daily smoothies. Simply go and buy some green vegetables and fruits, throw them all together into a juicer or blender to make a nutritious delicious smoothie. The color of your smoothie can resonate with the body's chakras. The color green, for example, resonates with the heart chakra, which is our central chakra. Empowering this chakra will create clarity into your aura and energy field. You can effectively make smoothies of any color, to help empower your body's natural intelligence.

Many resources are available for various recipes to help make the most nutritious shakes. Find the ones which suit you best!

Stimulants such as caffeine are over-stimulating for empaths. This external source of energy is so easily absorbed by sensitives that it can cause mental confusion. For most of my life, I felt I had an attention disorder as I was unable to hold my attention for long periods of time, it was only through realizing that I was incredibly sensitive to the food I was eating that I was able to clean up my diet. This allowed be get a handle on this mental short-coming and overtime gradually increase my ability to concentrate.

Empaths and sensitives, can sometimes struggle to be present with a high degree of focused concentration since they're easily distracted or stimulated by some external stimulus they pick up on. This makes it difficult to function at their best particularly in public places where they're surrounded by many people, such as schools or workplaces.

Being an empath requires a lot of close introspection through really understanding our bodies and how what we put into them impacts how we feel. Creating a journal is a great way to start to understand yourself and what works for you.

Practical exercises for Empaths

Shutting yourself from others is incredibly harmful psychologically for anyone, not just for empaths. This increases the sensitivity we feel when around others. We want to be able to function at our best in all situations and not become overly sensitive to 'regular' people.

A method many sensitives use unconsciously to stop the constant bombardment of others emotions and energy, is to distract themselves. Distracting works to lessen the impact of external stimulus. But there are various negative forms of distraction such as alcohol, drugs, sex, porn and junk food which can lead to a reliance or an unhealthy addiction. Most of these addictions shift our perception into a state where we are not as aware, this allows us to escape feeling the pain in the world. Try to avoid these at all costs!

In this chapter, we will look at positive exercises and forms of distraction which will help support you no matter what you're faced with without relying on unhealthy vices.

Using Affirmations

Many people use affirmations nowadays, they have become incredibly popular in all walks of life. They're positive statements repeated over and over to help us escape negative thought patterns while promoting positive ones. They can help keep an empath strong particularly in an overwhelming situation. You can create your own affirmations if something in particular resonates with you. Here are a few of the ones which I have found helpful -

'I refuse to absorb other people's energy. I can acknowledge how others are feeling, but I now shield myself from absorbing anything from them'.

'I can allow others close to me, without taking on their energy or emotions'.

'I feel and connect with my own feelings before anyone else's'.

Assertiveness tip –

Do you struggle saying no to people? This is a common occurrence among sensitives, here is an idea which I found helpful when presented with something I wasn't sure about. If for example, a friend of colleague asks you out for drinks in the evening, instead of agreeing immediately, respond with 'Ok, I will just have to check my schedule and let you know' - This isn't saying no! But it is in fact giving you some breathing space to decide whether or not this is something you want to do. With this kind of response, you don't feel like you have been put on the spot and that you must respond immediately. This gives you time to process the request and hopefully muster up the courage within to say no (if you don't feel like doing what was requested). Beginning to honor your feelings is incredibly important.

Here are three unfinished sentences which you can work with to help build your sense of boundaries. Try to come up with as many different responses as you can. By doing this you are gradually beginning to reinforce and develop stronger boundaries.

1) I have the right to ask for.........

Some answer here could include - space, respect etc.

2) To have enough time and energy to function at my best, it is ok to..........

Examples - refuse invitations, do my own work first etc.

3) If I refuse others, they may......

Examples - not like me, talk badly about me, respect me more etc

Without talking care of your own boundaries, you are effectively hindering yourself from living a happy and successful life. That's what it comes down to. Over time, this becomes easier. Helping others at your own expenses is detrimental to the whole.

Exercise

Exercise is an absolute must. I have personally found it to be one of the main tools I use that helps me enjoy life as an empath. The right training will not only exercise the physical body but the nervous system also (the root of your sensitivity). By exercising to engage the nervous system, we can almost reset our minds and bodies. This is exactly how I feel after a workout, as though someone has pushed a button and I have been energetically reset. It works incredibly well to clear away negative or any stagnant energy. It also increases the flow of freshly oxygenated blood all around the body. These are just some of the many benefits associated to exercise.

Another important tip is to stay away from public mirrors. The ones you find in gyms and clothes shops. Empaths can pick up negative energies being reflected to them from mirrors especially if the people who have been looking at their reflections are egotistical or self-absorbed. The empath can often take on this negative energy as their own.

Clearing your energy to create healthier boundaries

Reduce negativity - Due to our sensitive nature, we pick up negativity very easily. To help overcome this, empaths should start distancing themselves from negativity as much as possible. This can include people you know, certain places, even the news and social platforms. The TV and social media can really impact the empath on a subconscious level, they may not realize it at the time but they are picking up a lot of negativity from these sources particularly from the news, world affairs, soap operas and even reality TV shows.

Balance - Living a balanced life, is important for anyone, none more so than for an empath. This includes all areas of life such as diet, work, health, sleep, exercise etc. Keeping all aspects in some kind of balance help help avoid becoming over stimulated. Try not to overdo it, as you'll likely need longer to recover. I have personally found I can only exercise 2-3 times a week, any more than this and I tend to feel burnt out. Taking adequate rest is also important and will improve your overall health and well-being.

Determine what is not yours –

Sometimes we walk into a room or a situation and feel like we have energetically picked up a mood or a vibe which wasn't ours. Try to bring your conscious awareness to any feelings you suspect don't belong to you. If you don't feel it is yours then make a choice to discard it, send the unwanted energy away and down into the earth. This can be done easily, simply holding your focus and stating the intention in your mind while visualizing the emotion leaving you.

Declutter –

Since empaths fundamentally must claim ownership over their own energetic space and stop others intruding in it, they should also take the same care with their physical areas. If you are messy, untidy or have a lot of clutter, take the time to clear your physical space, doing this will clear your mind and energy also. Negativity tends to breed in clutter and mess.

Crystals for protection –

Crystals are a gift and a spiritual super power for promoting self-care. Anything can be used as a symbol of protection whether that is a piece of jewelry or a crystal. The most important thing is that you believe in whatever you are trusting for your protection. This belief alone will help protect you. People find it easy to trust in crystals due to their natural Earthly healing properties and they're fairly inexpensive to buy. If you are interested in learning in depth knowledge on how to use crystals and how to get the most out of these powerful stones then please check out my other book - <u>Crystal Healing: Heal Yourself & Transform Your Life</u>.

Now we will take a look at some crystals which work incredibly well as protection for empaths and sensitives.

Rose Quartz

This is a great crystal for empaths to possess simply for its grounding properties. It is often referred to as the 'Love Stone', since is resonates and works to repair the heart chakra. These qualities give the user a boost while helping to keep others negative emotions out of their space. It promotes all types of love, such as self-love, romantic, unconditional and platonic. Since it is a quartz, this means it has a high energy that can help bring a positive loving vibration into almost all circumstances. By bringing more love into an empaths daily life, it helps to lower stress while carrying warmth to everyone who is present. It is also used to improve self-esteem and attract genuine love into our lives. All these positive qualities bring balance to the emotions while helping to reduce stress and anxieties.

Black Tourmaline

This has been referred to as the 'must have' crystal for empaths. Known for its protective qualities this crystal enables the carrier to shield and deflect away any negative or low vibrational energies. It does this by processing any bad energy which comes into the auric field whether it's from other people or the environment. It also acts as a filter to protect us, which only allows good energies in, such as love, joy and kindness.

When carried regularly it neutralizes and purifies our own negative thought patterns by filtering them into positive energy. It is renowned as an extremely effective grounding stone, it achieves this by creating a connection between the body and Earth. This contact helps to align and balance the energy centers (chakras) while channeling positive healing energy through the whole physical body.

Sugilite

This crystal comes in a striking violet color and resonates with the 7th chakra - the crown. It creates a firm impermeable bubble around the carrier which helps protect them from negative energies of the environment and unwanted thought forms from others. It's incredibly effective at preventing energetic attacks from energy vampires by dissolving the bad energy patterns headed our way. Its power enables the user to go through their daily activities with a sense of inner strength and grace. Due to its activation of the crown chakra, it helps bring healing light in from the head down to the 1st chakra - the root. This influx of positive energy promotes balance and well-being that keeps us strong when faced with negativity.

Lapis Lazuli

A very popular and attractive stone that has been used for many thousands of years, particularly prevalent with the ancient Egyptians. It is best known for its protective qualities and its ability to repair, seal and strengthen the auric field. This helps in dissolving any negative emotions or energies which have been picked up. Lapis is a crystal of truth which helps increase self-awareness within the empath, with this we become more conscious of what belongs to us and what doesn't. In the same way, it allows what doesn't belong to us to be released and 'brought to the surface'. Lapis works with the third eye chakra, which is the seat of perception, with this we are able to gain clarity and 'see' exactly what is occurring around us energetically. Although, empaths sense this, they do not always clearly understand what is happening. It also helps promote grounding and restores balance.

Breathing Techniques

The 4-7-8 method

Every empath should possess at least one breathing technique in their tool box, the most popular one I use it called the 4-7-8 breathing method. This comes from Yoga and is often used to help reduce anxiety.

1) Place the tip of the tongue onto the roof of your mouth, right behind the top front teeth. This allows the muscles in your face to relax. You must keep your tongue in this position for the whole exercise. The technique can be performed in any position, standing, lying or sitting down. If used while sitting down, ensure the feet are planted firmly on the ground while sitting up straight.

2) Once in a suitable position. Breathe out all the air in your lungs out through the mouth.

3) Next, close the mouth, and begin to inhale deeply through the nostrils while mentally counting to 4.

4) Hold the breath for a count of 7.

5) Exhale the breath out from the mouth while counting to 8.

6) Repeat this breath cycle for 4 times. This shouldn't take much longer than 30 seconds.

This quick technique naturally alters our state into a more pleasant consciousness. It promotes a sense of relaxation especially when practiced a few times a day. For sensitives who struggle to sleep, this method can help relax you into sleep very quickly. It can also help reduce the fear response of fight or flight within the body, which naturally reduces anxiety and any stress related hormones.

Releasing Negative Emotions –

Empaths and sensitives are naturally emotional and therefore they're more susceptible to crying. This isn't necessarily a bad thing however, as this tendency can be used to help clear out negative emotions. When we work on ourselves through studying, reading, meditations, therapy or by whatever means, the old unwanted energies need to detach and be released from our physical bodies. These old energetic patterns can be let go off through crying, this is a healthy way to release. I am not suggesting crying all day and night, but letting the tears out once in a while, will do more good, than keeping them locked in. You can even try to invoke crying by watching a sad movie or listening to a song which you find deeply moving, this will usually trigger the release of any unwanted energetic pain. Crying is a natural human process and something which should be seen as necessary and healthy. We have been lead to believe that crying is a weakness when in fact it is a sign of strength which will only make us stronger and more emotionally robust.

During a bout of crying, feel as though you're letting go of old unwanted things and see yourself growing into something greater. This makes the very act of crying a positive empowering ritual.

Use crowded places

As we know, empaths and sensitives don't like being out in public places for too long. This problem can be approached in a different way however. We can use busy places as practice in developing our boundaries. When in a packed area, envision your boundaries constricting inward around you and completely shielding you from all negative external energies. We are effectively using public places as a training ground for learning to set boundaries. This is much more effective than practicing setting boundaries when you're alone at home.

Also, by going out with someone you are energetically compatible with (family member, partner or friend), acts as a further defense to your boundary. Both you and the other persons' energy will create a stronger shield around both of you. Further helping to distract and dispel any unwanted energies. You may have noticed that you do not feel as drained when out with a friend in public. This also works to distract you from external stimulus, as your focus is naturally more on the person whom you are with.

Yoga Poses

Yoga is ancient art form which has been used for many years to help empower people. We can use it in helping to create stronger boundaries around ourselves. The best poses for empaths are generally the ones which allow us to open up the body and reclaim our space. By holding these positions and breathing deeply into them before going out, strengthens our energetic space and aura.

Some of the best poses for this include, the star fish pose, this involves standing up straight with your legs and arms spread out wide. The other popular pose is called the warrior pose. Both of these poses make you take up space with your body, the space you take up is your energetic area. By doing these poses before heading out, you are setting your boundaries and stopping anything unwanted coming in. By expanding your aura and energy field in this way, you may become more noticeable, but you will feel much safer also.

Warrior Pose

Music/Audio

Listening to music through headphones while out can be greatly beneficial to help distract from the constant barrage of stimulus around you, providing you have done the work of setting a firm energetic boundary prior. Listening to audio can be extremely effective because it directs your focus inward to what you're listening to. I have personally found audiobooks the most beneficial as I can concentrate on what is being said. With music, I sometimes tend to switch off. Although both are effective, find what works best for you. Audio helps to further strengthen your boundaries since only you can hear what's coming through the headphones, this automatically removes you from the energetic flow of everyone else and reinforces the protective bubble around you.

Comfort Zone

I believe that working with our comfort zone is one of the keys to long-term growth for empaths or anyone else, for that matter. Learning to push ourselves past what we feel comfortable with helps build inner strength. We can be sensitive and strong! Empaths often struggle to move out of their comfort zones for the simple fact it is more uncomfortable for them to do so, compared to non-empaths. No matter what the situation is, whether it is going out into public places, or speaking out when you would usually stay quiet, you must learn to go inward and muster up the strength to face challenges head-on. I wish I could tell you there was a short cut and that being an empath was all plain sailing but if you truly want to find real fulfillment in life you must step out of your comfort zone. Firstly, with small steps and then gradually build up as you gain momentum. All empaths have something they would like to do or achieve but have often allowed their sensitivity to hold them back. The only way through this resistance is through it. If there is something you have always dreamed about, I urge you to make this a future goal and with focused action and courage, trust that you will eventually reach this destination. It won't be easy but it will certainly be worth it. The confidence and belief this builds within, is unspeakable.

Healing Yourself

We often hear about empaths abilities to help and heal others. But to maximize this talent we need to be fully healed first. Thankfully, we not only have the intuitive ability to heal others but also any emotional wound or disease within ourselves also. How powerful of a healer you become depends on your intention, belief, imagination while living with an open loving heart and mind.

Many empaths wounds come from a lack of self-esteem and trust. Not just trust in others, but a lack of trust in themselves. They may have experienced hurt through a close loved one, which has created these wounds within them. If you are able to pin point which experience caused your biggest emotional wounds than that is a great place to start. If you're not sure, then trust your instincts, they will guide you in the right direction.

Rebuilding low self-esteem can be particularly difficult for empaths, especially as they put others needs ahead of their own. Beginning to realize that they do not need to sacrifice their own happiness for anyone else's is an important realization. You matter, your feelings matter just as much as the next persons. You may have felt that caring for others meant you should neglect your own needs so you could help those who need you.

But with this type of behavior, your kindness will often be taken as a weakness, which will cause others to walk all over you. Healthy relationships are based upon reciprocity, which involves giving and taking in equal amounts.

When viewing all your relationships, begin to give more attention to those people who acknowledge you and hold a healthy degree of self-love for themselves. This means staying away from narcissistic types and energy vampires. Once you make the intention to put yourself first, you naturally start withdrawing your energy from unhealthy relationships. You instead direct that energy into yourself and with those who are genuine and caring individuals. This helps to significantly decrease stress and any anxiety related to your personal relationships.

Returning another's energy

In this exercise, we will set the intention to send the others negative energy or emotion back to where it came from. First acknowledge if you feel any trauma, pain or negative energy that is weighing down on you. Try not to judge the person this has come from. Realize, that by taking on this person's feelings or emotions, you're not helping them. They need to experience their own emotions and learn to grow through them by overcoming their own pain. When taking on others emotions, we are effectively preventing them from growing and developing. You can simply return the energy to the sender by clearing your auric/energy field or set the intention and visualize sending these feeling back to them. Use your imagination, these feelings can take any shape or form which looks appropriate to you. The intention is the most important part of this exercise.

Psychotherapy

Talking therapy with a qualified practitioner is one of the most popular ways of emotional healing. It involves discussing any psychological disorders or emotional problems that we are experiencing with a registered professional. It works by allowing the patient to freely discuss and talk about their feelings, in order to gain a greater understanding of themselves, which leads to greater healing, relief from their problems and increased self-confidence.

It is especially effective for empaths, as it gives them a safe space to be heard where they won't be judged. Combining talking therapy with other healing modalities such as EFT (emotional freedom techniques), somatic therapy and breathwork can help amplify therapy's effectiveness. Using these various techniques together allows negative residual energies and trauma which has been stored in the body to finally be released. Empaths will take on and store a lot of trauma, from others as well as their own. By processing this through the mentioned methods, you can finally begin to let it go and put it all behind you. With this freedom from the past comes a brand-new enthusiasm for the future and a life you can truly enjoy. Healing begins to correct and reprogram limiting beliefs and any dysfunctional thought patterns.

Energy Vampires and Psychic Attacks

'Energy vampires are emotionally immature individuals who have the sense that the whole world revolves around them. They are almost incapable of seeing things from another person's perspective. They often lack empathy'

– PsychCentral (3)

Most sensitives have been around or come across energy vampires or narcissistic people at some point. Even after spending a few minutes in their company we often leave feeling violated and drained. In my experience, most emotional vampires are not aware of this trait within them but that doesn't help us not feel terrible in their company. Even though they may be oblivious to their own nature, most of them unconsciously recognize that being around an empath makes them feel better and more positive about themselves. For this reason, they can often cling to empaths because of the positive feelings they are able to gain from being in their presence. Due to an energy vampires overbearing personality, empaths often struggle against these types of energetic attacks because of their weak boundaries. Being around them can negatively impact their own ability to function well. After spending too much time with these people, our energy begins to diminish into negativity, whereas the energy vampire feels uplifted from taking positive energy from us. They essentially feed on others positivity. It is important to recognize if you feel depleted, stressed or drained around certain people as you're likely in the presence of a psychic vampire.

The Reasons Behind Vampirism & Narcissism

These people feel cut off from themselves and deep down feel unworthy of being loved which stops them from getting their own needs met. The only way they can get what they need is to take it from others. Due to their unconnectedness to themselves they are unable to find fulfillment within, so this void is then filled by stealing energy from other people. They prey on easy targets, i.e. those with weak boundaries who can easily to drained.

Energy vampires are often singled out for being evil and harmful but their actions are often unconscious. They don't know what they are doing. They are victims themselves, although this doesn't make it any easier on us. The paradox is that the energy vampire and the victim are similar on some level. They have been drawn together and that is why the vampire is able to attach to the victim through this identification. The opposites have attracted one another.

Narcissists are often attracted to empaths and people in healing or spiritual circles as these people are the most open and loving. This makes them easy prey for an energy vampire. They will usually stay attached to these people for a long time, due to the victim's non-resistance. On the surface it will probably look like a positive friendship.

It is also worth mentioning that while certain people are energy vampires per se, most people have some vampirism tendencies depending upon their mood. If someone you know, a friend perhaps, is going through a particularly tough time they may unconsciously reach out in an energy sucking way, as they seek an uplift in their mood. They probably won't realize they are doing this but empaths should be on their guard against it. Telephone calls are one of the main ways friends can steal your energy. If a friend calls you regularly to talk about their problems, you may want to emotionally withdraw and detach consciously from the conversation. Be there to listen but not to take on their negative energy. Over time your friend will probably recognize they do not get a boost from unloading their problems onto you, so will probably stop sharing their personal issues as much. This doesn't mean your friendship with them will end but you are just setting a boundary between what is yours and what is theirs. Remember that healthy relationships are based on balance and an equal amount of giving and taking.

Energetic Cording

The primary way I have found to disconnect from these people is to cut them out of my life and stop communicating with them altogether. Not in a malicious way, but instead to essentially release them through love and forgiveness. This can be incredibly difficult to do however, especially if it is someone close such as a family member or a work colleague we have to see each day. In these scenarios, we can disconnect from the other by cutting our energetic ties to them.

'Cording' refers to an energetic connection between two people. These connections are usually between certain chakras. For example, when a mother gives birth to a baby they're energetically connected via the first charka (at the bottom of the torso). The root chakra from the mother connects to the root chakra to the baby. It would essentially look like a line of light from one to the other, this a healthy positive cord.

Healthy energetic cords can also form between people who are not related, such as spouses, close friends or anyone you feel a connection too. However, these cord connections can also be forced by one person onto another. This type of cording is unhealthy and draining to the recipient of such an act.

For example, people often become attached to their ex-partners. Even after the relationship is over, we can sometimes still feel a connection to this person. It is possible that your ex-partner had created a cord into your system to remember and to stay in touch with you energetically. This enables them to experience a little bit of your energy. When your ex is thinking or remembering you, they are creating and reinforcing an energetic cord into one of your chakras, probably unconsciously. This is why, even after the relationship is over, we cannot stop thinking about the other person. They are connecting to us energetically. That's why it is important to heal your own energy to stop other people cording into you again.

Most energetic cording takes place on one of the torso based charkas (1 to 4) these include the sacral (above the groin area), the solar plexus (mid-belly), the heart or the throat chakra. If you feel an ache or sensation in any of these areas when around a certain person, become aware that they may be draining your life force from you. You can block this by simply placing your hands directly over the affected chakra to help break the connection. Often in difficult social situations, people will cross their arms over their bodies (usually unconsciously), this helps us feel safer and defend our energy in this position.

The reason another person is able to cord you is because your chakras are not strong enough and must be healed. When the chakras are unhealthy or unhealed it leaves them open for others to attach to. Psychic vampires gain a strong feed of energy from the chakra points. For example, a person I used to know would attach to my solar plexus and I could physically feel the sensation of the connection. When the chakras and boundaries are healed, healthy and established, it becomes difficult for others to form this connection though cording your energy field. Energetic cords form when we still carry hurt or baggage with us from our pasts. These wounds leave our chakras open so they become easily attachable. The low energy of this wound attracts the low energy of the vampire or narcissist.

Empaths often feel a sensation in their solar plexus region. This chakra is the seat of our emotions. This is where the emotions of others are most deeply felt and where we are the most vulnerable to be corded and drained. Weakness in this area can cause digestive system and stomach problems.

Cord Cutting Exercise

Toxic draining relationships require what is often referred to as cord cutting. Once energetic cords are established it can be difficult to break them without conscious intention. If you feel drained from certain family members, ex-partners, work colleagues or anyone whom you have close regular contact with then it may be time to repair your connection to them. You might sense that this other person sends you negative, harmful thoughts and energy, even when you're not close to them.

If you feel you have been corded then this cord cutting exercise will help release it.

1) Imagine the other person and envision a cord or tube connecting the two of you, from one of your chakras.

2) Next visualize a cutting tool (such as scissors or sword) slicing through and cutting the cord at your chakra point.

3) Ask for the other person's energy to be returned to them and yours to be returned to you. Visualize this in your mind.

4) Following this, ask yourself what negative belief you were holding which attracted this experience to you in the first place? With this realization, we begin to see that we are not innocent helpless victims but in fact we are attracting these experiences to us, for a chance to overcome and grow through them.

5) Realize your self-worth as an empath is not dependent on helping others. This is a common misconception which leads to us attracting the wrong relationships.

6) End the exercise by forgiving the other party and releasing them with love.

Meditation

If you have left an interaction with an energy vampire and feel drained, this is a great time to clear the connection. This can also be achieved through meditation.

1) Close your eyes and begin by making yourself comfortable.

2) Scan your body from the head down to the feet and pay attention to any attachments you feel. It shouldn't be too difficult to determine what part of the body you are being drained from.

3) Upon determining what part of the body you feel this connection too, look to see the shape or form of the connection. See a physical representation of this energetic attachment. To me, it looks like an energetic tube which sucks energy in.

4) Begin cutting the attachment away from you. Envision you have a sword made of light and see this sword cutting through these attachments which are then being released from your body.

5) Once the attachment or cord is removed. You must apply healing to the area by placing your hand over the chakra and send healing energy to the area. See the open chakra begin to restore. Allow it to heal and repair itself.

6) As the chakra is healed visualize a new vibrancy and boost of energy within it.

7) Send the other person's energy and attachment back to them. There is no harm in this, it was their stuff in the first place.

8) Scan your whole body again noticing if there are any other attachments or sensations. If you do sense something carry out the same detaching for the new area.

9) Finally, envision a white light surrounding and protecting you. This bubble of protection will always remain with you unless you decide to release it.

You can practice this meditation almost anywhere. At work, on public transport or anywhere you are able to go within for a few moments.

The key to dealing with psychic attacks from unhealthy people is simply becoming more aware. Often energy vampires appear friendly, attractive and charismatic, which draws us in. The fact that they show us attention usually allows us to let them close to us. It is not our responsibility to heal these people. At least, not until we have healed ourselves first.

The Gift

This 'gift' is often seen as a curse and much of this book has focused on many of the negative traits of empaths. But this was important to help you learn how to manage and understand yourself better, so you can step into this gift and use it to its fullest capacity. Many of the so called 'negative' traits are actually the positive ones as well, they're just viewed in a different light. It's like double-edged sword, with which we're looking to effectively negate the negative effects by transmuting them into positive benefits.

Empaths have had feelings of over sensitivity since birth. So from day one, their brains have been wired up through neural connections to compensate for their natural alertness and sensitivity. Neural pathways are connections all brains make through repeated action. The more we do something, the stronger the associated neural pathways become established within the mind and through repetition these actions eventually become a habit. For example, if you avoided eye contact with others from a young age because you felt a powerful hit of their emotions, your brain will have created the connections to avoid eye contact each time you come into contact with someone, until eventually it became an unconscious habit.

For this reason, many of the behaviors expressed by empaths are deeply ingrained within their psyche via years of repetition through defending themselves. It can be incredibly difficult to change these deep-seated behaviors and beliefs. The easiest way around this is to build upon the tendencies which are already present. Building upon established neural pathways with new connections will be the easiest way to reinforce new behaviors.

The first step is to fully own and accept this trait as a gift. It is the only way we can begin to harness the power it holds. For many years, I used to hate this trait. I did whatever I could to try and overcome it, wrongfully thinking that it was a psychological programming that I had picked up from my mother. But in fact, it was my mother's genetic predisposition towards sensitivity which had been passed down to me. I then realized I was stuck with it, through this I learnt to accept it as part of myself and how to work with it.

Fighting against it lead to some difficult challenges in my life from my earliest years. I was incredibly shy growing up, I was very sensitive to pain and easily distracted which lead to anxiety in my adult life. It was only through owning this part of myself that I was able to begin functioning at a higher level. Learning how to protect myself, allowed me to find more happiness. This is what I want for you. I know how difficult it can be being an empath, we often feel so different, so misunderstood, left out and not part of normal society. But, as I learnt, we are special.

MARIANNE GRACIE

You can start to understand these gifts more, by beginning to pay closer attention to yourself through non-judgement and non-resistance. For instance, I have had always an expansive aura which I hated, as I would always be noticed by others which was terrible for me since I was incredibly shy. I saw this as a negative part of myself. But as I learnt to work with this gift, I understood that I could affect the energy of an entire room with my presence. People would tell me I was kind and would be grateful for my attention. They would tell me deeply personal things, from only having met them for a few minutes. Sometimes they would even comment, 'why am I telling you this? I barely even know you'. Of course, I knew why they were opening their heart to me, it was because I was truly hearing what they had to say.

This is a gift which should be used through your own conscious decision. You decide if you want someone to unload their issues onto you. This is only achieved through setting boundaries. By doing this, I built my self-confidence up and started to trust myself more. Animals loved me. I discovered I was very visually creative, that I enjoyed writing and that I could communicate with others in a way which I had never known. I still continue to find out new things about myself all of the time, it's great! I genuinely believe the same is possible for each and every empath out there.

Your talents

The ability to connect with others better, to really put yourself into their shoes and understand where they are coming from is a trait of immeasurable value. This can be used in any number of professions from sales, to medicine to therapy. People with this skill will never struggle to find work. The world needs more genuinely caring and understanding people.

Empaths have a high degree of introspection. With their sensitivity, they can direct this power inward, towards themselves. This helps make them very intuitive, providing they can quieten their minds from any mental chatter. Learning to work and trust this intuition over time, will begin to guide your life in the right direction.

This sixth sense will make it easier to connect and discover your true calling in life, your deepest purpose. This can be a struggle for many people, but empaths usually have an in-built knowing about what they are capable of achieving and where their true passions lie. They may often need to develop the courage to go after their dreams but finding what they are here to do isn't usually a problem.

Healing

This is the natural ability to heal ourselves and others. To truly achieve this skill, we need to have developed and learnt to separate our emotions from others. Putting ourselves into another person's shoes while seeing and feeling what they experience is a treasure to behold. But it can be a difficult to handle. Being able to understand others in this way allows us to treat them with more compassion. By picking up on their history and their hurt we are able to become powerful transformative healers. Empaths are naturally drawn to professions which involve healing others, they can have great careers as therapists and in alternative healing methods such as Reiki practitioners, hypnotherapists and such.

They can also heal through feeling another's emotions. By getting in tune with another's pain, they help heal the patient through a combined transmutation of their emotional trauma. Connecting to the pain in another person, allows the skilled empath to draw this pain out of them (with the intention of the patient).

They can even help uncover hidden emotional issues through sensing others emotional blocks, then helping the person to begin working through them. In this way, they provide great guidance and help for directing inner healing. This skill is most effective if someone is stuck on a particular issue and requires guidance on how to move forward.

Telepathy/Psychic -

It is generally believed that everyone has a certain degree of psychic ability, which allows us to see into past or future events with which we have no connection too. This is usually done unconsciously, with little intention. But, when it happens, it usually leaves us in awe and shock. Unsurprisingly, since empaths are attuned to picking up on subtleties in energy, they also possess a natural talent for telepathy. They can correctly predict future events through a hunch which is referred to as precognition.

Empaths can function on various levels of psychic work, these can include Mediumship which involves working with and sensing spirits. Many also have a natural ability to connect with and understand animals on a deeper level, so professions which require working with animals can give them a lot of satisfaction.

Some use their abilities through a skill called Geomancy, this is where they have honed their abilities to feel the energies of the Earth. With this sense, they can order, detect and predict water flow and the weather.

It can be frustrating trying to understand why we have this ability while looking to uncover our life's purpose. But by using your natural talents, abilities and interests as a guide, they will help take you to your truth.

Help Raise the Vibrational frequency of the Planet

Just by our sheer presence on earth we help transmute negative energies, without even knowing we are. This alone makes us indispensable. Empaths mop up the crap created by others, especially in times of huge negativity. Increasing the vibration of the planet is essentially Gods work or at least a highly spiritual undertaking.

We can increase our ability to do this through self-love and caring for ourselves first. By nurturing all of our health we promote our natural talents and then by following our interests, the path ahead begins clear, this adds positive vibrations to the planet. If whatever you do is from a place of love, you will always find happiness.

You'll notice a big shift when you start to look towards thriving in this world, instead of just being in survival mode (which is what most of us have been used to). Being brave enough to take the steps in the direction of your goals and dreams, is when the real magic begins to happen. So instead of always seeing your gifts as a hindrance, start to move into their true power.

I personally believe empaths have a great strength because of what they have already had to endure through life, the pain and the hurt. This strength which has built up should be harnessed and used to propel you forwards to conquer new heights while positively impacting the planet.

6th sense

Empaths view of the world through their sensing emotions, feelings and energies effectively creates within them a 6th sense. If it was taken away from us, we would most probably be left feeling stuck. We would lose so much of what this gift gives us and what we also take for granted, as we predominately focus on its negative aspects. Being able to tell when someone is lying or telling the truth or being able to sense others pain and if they need healing are all forms of guidance.

Sometimes our help will be dismissed which can be upsetting especially when we see another person hurting. But some people need to experience their suffering to allow them to grow and awaken so they can create a better life for themselves. It is their journey. If there was no resistance, there would be nothing to force us to grow stronger. Difficult circumstances can sometimes be seen as an insurmountable mountain, but they must be tackled head on. Overcoming these challenges might be painful and difficult, but the view from the top of the mountain along with the inner gold you will discover, makes it all worthwhile.

Conclusion

Congratulations! I am incredibly proud of you for making it to the end of this book. It truly lets me know that there are people are out there who are genuinely interested in reaching their fullest potential, this is something the world needs more of. I am convinced that if each and every empath on our planet learnt more about how to harness this special gift and bring it out, then the world we live in would look very different. We are needed here and have great work to do, with that comes a great responsibility and we can only take this on by first taking care of ourselves. Once we know how to do this, only then can we extend and reach out to help others on their journey.

It is important to remember that everyone's experience of life is different. So it is important you begin to look within yourself for more answers and recognize that the keys to change begin with you. Look at your life as a fun journey of self-exploration. If someone were to ask me now, if I would change my empathic nature, the simple answer would be no. I have learnt to work with and embrace all the gifts it has given me, without this ability I wouldn't be me.

I hope by using the knowledge in this book you're able to find more joy and fulfillment in your daily life. Everyone deserves to be happy but for some of us this can be more challenging. Stepping into your power and making a commitment to improve your life, is the single most important thing in creating change. So look within for your courage. If there is one thing I have learnt from being an empath, that is that we are incredibly strong and can endure a lot. It is about time we started to direct this strength towards creating a happier and more joyful life for ourselves.

Once you learn to work with this gift, you will experience more incredible moments than you have ever known. A fully engaged empath, who knows how to manage their gift, can be so fully absorbed in reality that every moment becomes pure joy. Reaching this level takes dedication and work but with practice you'll experience the bliss of living a full life. Feeling every moment is the key to real joy and happiness.

Thank you!

Resources

1) Social cognition in social anxiety: first evidence for increased empathic abilities. Tibi-Elhanany Y[1], Shamay-Tsoory SG. (2011)
2) http://www.briantracy.com
3) https://psychcentral.com/blog/.../11/.../how-to-avoid-being-drained-by-energy-vampires
4) http://naturalfamilytoday.com/health/6-effective-grounding-techniques-for-empaths/

Made in the USA
Middletown, DE
01 September 2017